Spiritual Aberrations

Thoughts, illusions and aberrations on the path to spiritual awakening for Yogis and Buddhists.

Shiva Bodhi
Spiritual Aberrations

Herstellung und Verlag:
BoD – Books on Demand, Norderstedt

ISBN: 9783754327166

Disappear

Have well understood and have a clear opinion,
ignore the discarded monkeys for a short time, the
kicked thoughts do not have to take over,
tomorrow is also another day. We believe in
miracles, miraculous coincidences and divine
chance. The day after tomorrow will bring
salvation, take heart and strike your r restlessness,
fill your lungs with pure alpine air and look at your
life. And like the image and love and fight like an
opinion maker, believe in values and do not see
crazy monkeys as brothers. We mean that, and
need that very much, and yet will disappear too
quickly.

Give me a kiss

Obviously I aged, quickly and without having done
great things, still dreaming of the big day, no one
can know what will happen to me and maybe you.
The shopping carts at our place were always more
than full, the indomitable pose once again and are
not seen. The world responded quite well to me,
but never ordered special things or asked for
anything. There is nothing to ask, the expansion of
consciousness does not tickle and who wants to
discover the day with us. Time passes almost too
slowly, catching up with oneself is impossible.
Confided secrets are divulged as always and the
most intimate becomes the joke of the day. The old
also bring nothing, the young think of the moment
or not at all, and already again reteach and mope
and no longer necessarily want to be there. Hide
well and no one will find you, a sadness, a laugh of
a spectator, hope never dies, so they say. The
horror came with the hangover, the toilet bowl was
too far away and the hunger will probably be gone
for the next while, and the know-it-all continued to
watch over the essentials and quickly joked once. I
feel sick. Horribly nauseous. Without manhood
there is no sense in displaying it and the roosters
talked, powerless, about the future. Everything

slipped away, the finger pointing and the head shaking. Again nothing was understood, for whom also. Give me a kiss.

Hear you

Take care of you
Won't wound you
Have no head
For all the thoughts
You sing a song
And fly through the air
Good words describe
Hit you right in the heart
Lift you up
There's so much to hear
The ear is unfortunately closed
Conversations remain
And
Do you see me
Or
Do I hear you

Remains

You're already a little crazy, kneading at old wounds and suddenly you get up and walk away, everything has become too much and self-will needs no discipline, be proud of it, stir in the mud at home, insult the primal mother and lie down, pull the thick blanket over your head and ask what's wrong, the heavy blanket squeezes the air out of you and you stammer about freedom, the crazy becomes more intense in you, the sentences longer and the goodnight music sounds beautifully from the radio, hours pass and slowly you dive into sleep, the self-will remains.

And the day is wasted again

All that is, must not be
And in me is an is
Told me so many times
We took it and we have it good
We ask and start a having
And no longer meet the guessing
It is the being but not in the I
Have lost little by little the I
Am wide awake and accompany the day
Without sense there is no here
Dreamed and felt a faithful brain
Nothing has happened
Nothing is as thought
And the day is wasted again

The end is already near

I'm tired of worrying
We play too well
Believing in the beginning and the end
To have loved deep in the heart
The right attitude plays the greatest role
To play with the days
And death comes with you
The butt itches
To hear a familiar laugh
I pocket the having
The end is already near

Or do you have me and are popular

Lust is already overflowing
Love affairs are lost
Bleeding hearts are seen
Balanced missteps are forgotten
Am caught in me and in your thoughts
Pain enchants the day
Feels the parting only softly
Good feelings are not always good
Be a better man and rule me
To lead with lowest urges is the art
And shout out the pain of life
If you give yourself, I believe
It's a mindful urge
Or have me and be popular

The search and the attempt

The sun has set, relatively quickly it has become
cold, the nonchalance has faded. In the
conversations some things turn out, especially
those who were rarely allowed to talk, told about
the warm day and now meant very cheeky and did
not really have an indulgence. So I listened and did
wrong and very interested, my ears could not open
and the brain said curfew. And the sound waves of
the otherwise mute did not really reach me. So I
couldn't think about anything and was too lazy to
do so. The eternally old, rehashed stories, they
already reeked of antiquity, there were no new
experiences, and the pants got tighter and tighter.
What a dog, I thought, a smart dog that thinks like
a cat and eats like a pig. The favored ones thought
they were lucky and really attributed everything to
their talents, self-confident you have to be,
otherwise you train it and talk yourself into it, then
you can get somewhere. And the know-it-all didn't
stop, I was just along for the ride and I was and am
a failure. And I like being a failure. Life goes on and
thousands of mouthpieces are desperately looking
for ears, thinking of no brain to process at least
parts. Answers are not wanted, discussions are not
needed and understanding can be a joke. A dog

trying to manipulate me, a pig eating like a nervous sow. The brain bleeds, the greatest story is awarded, so please think. In itself, a well-invented lie does nothing, no hurricanes will hit you, and you yourself probably will not notice. But the tender love in your tense heart is still looking for something, a piece of the longed-for happiness. Everything will be different again, and the questions whether they should and you want will not end. But it does not matter. Everything is always new, perceive yourself, no matter how, and you will shine like a bacon rind, look joyfully in the belly and doubt. Look for it and try it.

Certainly have drummed well

Thrown off track
Seen from a different angle
Does the benefit remain
Or will
No one thinks anymore
Superiority loses its meaning
We feel a burning in the back of our minds
And sniff our way through
What else can we show
Kindness and compassion
Want to be praised
To beg for attention
To be ready at any time
And be the beloved helper
Sure to have trumped well

Go home and become the night

Have dreamed the days
Again
To discover the meaning in the days of tomorrow
Nothing is left of the gain
And the night has fallen
The all-knowing gaze took on a rigidity
The night brought cool air
The wish was not really fulfilled
The text was misunderstood
And there is nothing left to read
So everything goes round in circles
Well called
All understood
Go home and become the night

Raised to look to the near future.

Ran at full speed, pulled in the belly and beamed at the tired faces, our commonality is promoted, the good and a reasonable education. Aging no longer has any meaning, and the steeled lower legs do not remain free of varicose veins. Where is the world going, I'm in. My hat has a wide brim and the felt is of the finest, I don't mind the sun and I am ready for more humiliation. With my head held high, I contemplate the near future.

Sense makes that

Lost in the darkness of principles, have land and gold enough and often stand by and wait. Relying on social feelings, themselves do not live differently and kiss the world, just be neat. As it went well with the conceit, we could afford more than the average. Many congratulated us and slashed our car tires at night, understand well is the basis of friendship. So I take off my hat and greet the round, meet friendly faces and reap the great thanks. The thanks for nothing. Prepare the evening well, cook a good soup and take my notebook, read up. It makes sense.

And are also sometimes lost

What truth is there
Have you met them while walking
Nothing but dirt and whipped cream remains
The intended answers are harder to find
Always reinvented
Not consciously lying
Nor know the truth
And ever get lost

Are

The dirty fingernails just do not look nice and think
about washing and cleanliness and can look
forward to the future again or are there also
opposite voices in you and do what you always
wanted and scream with joy and give yourself and
are.

This is how it is

The goat goes home
The child grows older
The big man falls apart
Affections are exchanged
Accepted and lost
Well greeted and warmly received
The worms eat their way through the head
The heavenly song grows fainter
Where are you
Are you already asleep
You disappear into the darkness
Everything seems silent and lonely
And so it is

And the church bells are ringing

You have already eaten your fill and are still greedy
for more, your stomach is already well filled, but
your tongue is licking for more. There is something
beautiful about encounters. Joyfully excited you
chat with opponents, grandma is buried and bacon
tastes the same as always. The days are coming and
the earth will be your final resting place. Maybe
there will be no more bacon and maybe the
children will laugh even louder than you do now.
Don't get sentimental, there's nothing left and the
next ones need space. And the church bells are
already ringing.

And sometimes well attended

The day has not started for a long time
At least I think so
The shoes press on the toes
They should be one size too tight
It hurts and distracts me
My face is distorted
And you're sorry you're struggling
There's no coming together
Come here and hug me
It won't do any good, but it's nice
Make friends and find something good in the hour
The trapped time flees in haste
And yet can catch nothing
Have hoped forever
Again many things in the day to fathom
And sometimes well attended

And yet you lose yourself

What do you want to understand, the system of nature or your dearest counterpart, or yet yourself, reach into your backpack and take out your sandwich. You will find the right pattern and you will not want to do anything with it. Use the artifice of different ways of looking at things and slip from one person into another. For example, take a selfie and start singing a nice song, show yourself almost naked and still you won't be noticed. Then start running and grab as much luggage as possible to have more with us and be happy to have hoarded it. I tie myself up and ask once in this confinement and hear nothing and still do not feel uncomfortable. The self-shines beautifully and believe again in the higher, similar to all, and mine to understand and feel happy. And you eventually lose yourself.

And you are dead

Was suffocated
Cold becomes the skin
The tip of your nose slowly turns blue
The day tasted sweet
Love gives itself to me
Can't stand anything more
And have a hard time
The smell becomes pervasive
A shudder goes obliquely over the observers
Opinions come alive
The sweat tastes disgusting
And one is dead

Too deep

After the many conversations I fell asleep and tried
to take in the new truths, I also wanted to say
something, but no one listened to me or said
anything about my opinion. The deep sleep
recovered me and the voices became quieter,
actually I didn't understand anything either,
nevertheless I wanted to have my say and be there.
Many sentences were said, especially about the right
behavior for more understanding of the others. I
also felt sick, for example from the bottom to the
top, from the wet lips and the spit that flew
through the air. I can whistle for the hoped-for
kindness, sleep is the best remedy. I take a sip of
liquor, I feel sick, and look kindly and deeply at the
pile of words. Too deep.

Sense

Finally a thought with sense and very short and
pointed and yet escape and empty the mind and
take a deep breath and get it as a gift, the artificial
sense.

Disengage and slip off

The chest feels neatly constricted, some things have
not been clarified and lie heavy from stomach to
throat, it will be a start again and I treat myself to
an ice cream. Greetings are no longer in my nature,
dialogues leave a bad taste, and I loosen up. My
ulterior motives are drowning in the morass of
many views, yet I enjoy lapping up the ice cream
and wonder if the restlessness is getting better.
Tomorrow you may take a deep breath and make
new plans for your life. Detach yourself and slip.

Particularly reassuring is the farewell

There I ran along and shouted funny sayings to my
counterparts, the attitude slackened a little, the
running makes tired. Whether the stove is still on
or already off, no one sees and it will certainly be
even hotter. I listened then nevertheless still and
marveled not badly, over the well rhymed
statements and hard sayings. In the stomach it
growled and the hunger dominated my head. So the
madness could begin, important things in the
environment and a small dominating thing. A good
start in this environment. Particularly reassuring is
the farewell.

Everything has a meaning

The ear is clogged by the many words
Mouths move towards you
Know nothing of tomorrow
Affection is also an inclination
Stand up again
Everything has a meaning.

Let

Falling over and gasping for air in the earth, briefly discussing but somehow not being heard, mouth chewing wet mud, the day joyfully echoing in my heart and lying to me, fingers drilling holes in the ground and just letting the day be day.

And we continue to search

We have locked everything new in our hearts
Come here and find my happiness
Gladly I give you a piece
After hours well fed and hungry
I won't be full today
Nor thirst there's no end
We humans become wild
Thunderstorms do not irritate us
The bloody nose was beaten
And the roaring gets on our nerves
All friends were lost
And we continue to search

Future

Be against it and think of a good phrase and shout
it out without fear and slowly wake up and float
into a sweet future.

And go when you want

Happy constraints
Will not be bad
Have received
Have answered
Take care
Nothing will get worse
It is
And leave when you want to

The beginning is made again

Sit up and see better
No longer being alone
Greet and perceive
Eyes meet eyes
A brief embrace
A tear fertilizes the earth
Being perceived
The beginning is made again

At

Spoiled by being, I confess myself ofttimes and make a plan, there is a mountain I will climb and then I will understand myself or not and am here and rub the dirt from the interstices and am.

The nest is empty

Frozen through, I lie in the trickle and count my
fingers through, everyone is there and seems tired.
The night was cold, the encounters did not go
cheerfully and the spirit of wine weighed me down,
there was not much to say. Enjoyed properly and
proud of it, drank properly and proud of it. Proud,
really proud and happy. Well-aligned days damn us
and freedom, how to find the good, in drinking and
eating and being a pig. The relationships that please
and the big gulp and be right and stay true to the
line. Religious sense finders but off and bite their
nails, orders that must be obeyed and laugh
through the rest of the day. Cold stagger home and
look for the door key The nest is empty.

The chant sounds high.

The leg was peed
The trouser pipe hangs heavy
The wetness takes the cold
Casual crumbles quickly
The leg loses its meaning
I run into a wall
And beat my nose bloody
All beginnings are hard
Slowly the pants dry
And slowly the blood dries on my face
The conversations get louder again
Everybody joins in
And talk wildly together
The past disappears
The song rings high.

Being disabled

Chopped off spinners lie in the bowl for the day's meal. Vanity proliferates and brings out thick ulcers, the sun grills the brown raised facial contours black. Cold it gets in the back where no one looks, and all questions are quickly answered, guilty of nothing, relying on a good opinion, or deeply believing in a good opinion. The heart you do not need to close, be ready for all feelings, for I like to say that I live and also stumble. But be vain, be blackened and breathe deeply. Spit the phlegm out of your lungs, it's not all as we thought after all. Be disabled.

How well can you wait

Spit on the face
Cake on the buttocks
Yodeled up and smiled at
We fraternize fast
Time has caught us
Who'll hold a grudge
How are you
How well can you wait

Days and evenings pass

We will see
What will make us happy
Want to breathe deeply again sometime
Drugs numb us
Nothing to lose
Everything stays the same
We meet in neutral space
Wake up and think
There is nothing to understand
Cancel all the times
Days and evenings pass

Entangled

The teetotalers join together and have come up
with new slogans, want to unsettle well, are in the
good right and take everything on themselves and
know no mercy, crazy and normal and entangled.

What is then

To have a good idea of what is beautiful, above all
tall and slim and then funny and nice and then
young and unspoiled and preferably wealthy. The
swamp affects us all, he thought, still stuck. Good
character was all but forgotten, and his own strong
personality, needing that character. Deeply sucking
in the leaden air, he nodded opinionatedly, his
index finger holstered, waiting for the opportunity.
What then.

There is no mercy

Be cordial with opinions, shout apart is something
simple and I know you. Frighteningly large
becomes the opposite and the grace does not exist,
everything sinks. The rain is part of it, the silence
carries the main part of the mood, beautiful and
ugly, it feels good. An earworm repeats endlessly in
the head. There is no mercy.

And finally resign

My chafed feet need a bath
The calluses soften
Start to breathe and live again
Nothing is free and you have to pay
Care for the slowly dying body with sensitivity
I wait for you and you do not come
And the believed freedom does not exist
Still believe in it
And grow old in the process
The feet are slowly wrinkling
The heat rises in my head
I have not been happy for a long time
Friends ring my doorbell
I don't listen and my feet dissolve
The self-confidence is lost
The whole being collapses
Even strong thoughts are no help anymore
And the fun comes to an end
And finally resign

Or yet further

A remarkably great mind does not give up
Does not take other fine minds for a ride
Listening is a courtesy
Soon it will be over
Find the good hour
What have you to ask
Do not lose your counterparts
Or they will close
Or they will open

A fertile head world

From the earth shoots the weeds and also the lettuce, have added enough fertilizer and are ready for anything. The cramp in the left side of the face slowly subsides, perhaps unintentionally sucked on the artificial fertilizer and got sick. That's the way it is, the game with the rich harvest, not everything is always perfect, want to have more is the basis. Look at the wildly sprawling field, massage the already almost dead half of your face and start a discussion with the advocates of the never saturated. They buy into you, want to see interest and quickly give up the good face. Win and lose even faster, get a cramp in the other half of your face or even in your heart, but don't destroy yourself completely or you won't be able to pay interest. And the belief in the mundane quickly disappears, you also no longer know the past, the business counts and the lucky charm is the fertilizer. Strengthen your life and find new network partners, help each other, life brings unspeakable profit and small pains will be already to bear. A fertile head world.

From

There I dared not say anything to myself and hid
and enjoyed my life, always sniffing my own stench,
the bliss is perhaps there, in the back, in the middle
of the darkest hole and count off the thoughts and
live me out.

Find

Trick and manipulate with words and capture those who are vulnerable and find hope for a glorious future with words.

Or are you already quite

You wake up briefly in the night, look at the alarm
clock and see a blur of time that you immediately
forget. The unsolved problems of the day twitch in
the muscles, thinking through is no longer
necessary, you stand on the fast world and do quite
well in terms of success The few dark figures you
can gladly compare with yourself and the higher is
also studied intensively. Be conversational and have
a quick answer ready at all times. Forget your
loopholes, as of tomorrow you have none and are
not yet full. Or are you already full.

For the silence is appropriate there

The spirits have flown away
All alone I stand in the house
The dark sky does not show the stars
And the illusions show stronger
A single ghost remains
And he is afraid of reality
Only no one knows reality
And is always new
Ghost hands reach out and touch
The upper eyelid begins to twitch violently
One twitch and you've won
For silence is appropriate there

Die slowly

Accept and squeeze
Being cornered
Being especially unfree
To have again forever
We do not see you
Eternity remains
And the having
Give the opinion
Or will you stay alone
Nothing helps you
Talk to you
Teach you
And then hide
Slowly die

The stomach growls

The ear itches, the earwax seeks its way out, the
anticipation of the wonderful feast brings a bit of
happiness to the little heart. Invent a personality
and add authority and a typical kind of doer check
to it. This way you will survive and positive
thinking will take over you, if any depression or
even anxiety comes, forget about it, life is ruled by
the mind, no matter and in which direction. Or not.
The stomach growls.

And a new beginning

The sniffles do not go away
The snot runs over the upper lip into the mouth
There was nothing else
We will see
A kindness sends its regards
You have not yet discussed the highest
The ailments in the back plague again
And the biting does not get better
Goodness returns
Old sufferings just stick
There are no limits in the head
Or does the space shrink daily
The friendly ones proudly pass by
And a new beginning

And the respect increases

The short-cut meadow lay there like a fur, lying
down you had the feeling to be safe, the insects
gave rest, the ticks held a midday nap. Sharp
observers were out of the air and the sun kindly
burned everything unprotected, the day was good
to bear. Fellow travelers showed their best side and
made themselves small, threw compliments at us
and showed us that we are poor worms. No matter
and yet strange, the envy no one should really want,
certainly not the target, or better the target. Put
your hand in your pants bag and try to look casual,
the pants are too wide and look very cheap. Throw
a spell and you will succeed, sit wide-legged and
show an apparent untouchability. Nothing
succeeds. And the respect increases.

And hopefully does not turn blue

The trail is erased
The insects buzz around like crazy
There's no rest
And swallow a fly
It does not satisfy
And there's nothing to tell
A bad feeling lingers in the throat
The tongue feels furry
The fly keeps buzzing in my stomach
And I have a thirst for liquor
Memories fly at me
Summer will be hot
Insects will thicken the air
And seek refuge in open mouths
Everything is well thought out
Swallow fast and forget the bite
The head is still white
And hopefully will not turn blue

What a sentence

Great flashes of thought hang up the view of life,
you swallow and talk to yourself, there can be
nothing to it or yet, there I argue with myself and
love does not know itself, and the evening redness
is lost in talking. What a sentence.

Or the evening of life

Good sayings have knocked
Well learned from books and often heard
You can do many things
And in the end nothing remains
Maybe a good saying on a tombstone
Or a hint from someone
Gather many things and build an altar
Seek allies in madness
And bless the places of worship
Who are your friends
Where will they go with you
Will they love you and love each other
Or will they only think with you
The beard is long and very old
Everything must be right and you will find yourself
Or not find
The golden heart shall not be weighed
Time stands still
Everything has a name and therefore seems good
With or without, it doesn't matter
It is the young morning
Or even the evening of life

Buttoned up

Well drunk looking for a brightness in the head and
I keep looking and find a lush piece of soft mass
and startle and feel a twinge in the stomach area
and see already eaten holes, reach deeper and
deeper and find a pliable legality well dressed and
very buttoned up.

Alone now

Simple conversations ripple along, one readily allows the opinion of others and laughs inwardly at it, fear comes soon enough. Things get better with rest, conversations become more profound and everyone forgets about the other. The heart pulses restlessly, the psyche triggers the descent and the disease begins to germinate. I got sick and the birds chirp a love song and attract the females. Fake conditions confuse the audience, the player doesn't know either and quick thoughts almost drive you crazy. Knowledge yes, but the knowledge is pure theory, since everything, as we already know, has been reinvented. Clouds approach in a rush, blacken the sky and wait for the big discharge, self-pity needs food and finds it everywhere. The stuffy nose begins to run, everything becomes lighter and the interlocutors have disappeared. Now alone.

And also nothing more thought out for the day

Hug me lightly and smell me
Your hand feels very wrinkled
The goal shall be found after all
And the spells will have an end
Or will have no end
Good friend, take the responsibility from me
Please yourself
And say goodbye quickly after your work is done
You will soon have no will of your own
To find it is a great art in itself
To unstop my ears and find peace
Feel bled dry and without a fresh start
It all started somewhere
Maybe read a good book
Didn't laugh at it
Thought something else through for the day

And look away

Fearful I always was
Then in war and now in war
Everybody likes to party
You and me and no big questions
Is the big break coming
Or does it just break through
The great community
With countless dependencies
Come with me
And suck it all up
And lose yourself

Out goes the day

A red moon goes with me
Illuminated and almost illuminated
A glow goes with me
Inside me it's getting dark
There is nothing to grasp
Can we grasp together
The hours are lost
The day goes out

Night

Fresh cool air flows into the night, cool our heads
and think now to see better, but it does not work,
with effort nothing shall get better and the coolness
does good, briefly look up and fall, in the middle of
the night.

Thank you and amen

My love is great
The pump is pumping strongly
Everything pulsates
The wind whistles through my pants
My forehead burns
Much withers
Self-talk sounds friendly
The sky winks and laughs
A lovely day
Disturbing confidences
Brought closer
Thank you and amen.

But the past is the past

My daily game with material stakes never ended and never brought happiness, why should. Just being on luck and not wanting anything more. You can't really use the word love there. Days passed and my heart grew weaker, restless life with no real challenges. The great challengers sat bitterly on their perches and sorted the world, steeled their being and quickly retreated. I crept into the privacy of the homeless and studied them, what do they have that I don't. Is my roof the panacea or is it starting to crumble too. I think so, my head is wet from acid rain. The hair sticks together greasily and the passing days were to blame, nothing comes back and the memory doesn't really do much either. Deep breath and reset, the highest and last bet and lose. But bygones be bygones.

Summer is already here

Relaxed look in the sun rays
It is warm and the day is good
Getting thirsty again and again
And I take a deep breath
Reach into my cash register
And buy a novelty
Found a lot
The future is none of our business
The songs are getting quieter
It's hot and I almost can't breathe
To be broken out
And scream with happiness
Summer is already here

This is good after all

The beard grows on my face, looks terrible, and I feel bad. Life hangs by a thread. Pity finds the love and tenderness, although then it brings something, just from the separation, just before the crash. Maybe it does. Well works the day with the trappings. I lean on the neighbor and tell about solutions not found, he does not listen. That's just as well.

Maybe also eat

Remain in need
To know is a way
To be especially lonely
To believe in finding remains
Not to let anything get worse
And guilt
Questions fade
Pleas remain
Hope is beautiful
To eat the Jell-O
Maybe eat it too.

All conversations in the head are then for the fishes

Emerge from the dark corner
The taste in your mouth feels bad again
Take a deep breath and cough away
The pain in your neck will subside one day
Hasn't someone been looking for you for years
Are you still at the beginning or do you already
know more?
It won't do you any good either way
Just take life easy
And you'll want some things
Start talking and really mean it
And it's got you again
All the talk in your head will be for the fishes

Or not

Preach truth without exception
Receive and read truth
Give everything to the best
Accusing and blaming
Getting fatter and also smelling bad
The sun burns the earth dry
All become more awake and friendly
Getting in touch with everything
And you will be taken in
Later you can tell others
Life has a good taste
And the givers receive you
Appreciate good connections
Show your lips and become even friendlier
Understand you
Understand me
Or don't

Are simple

The little man arrives and takes away his ego,
becomes a little kid and sticks knowledge up his
ass, everything becomes a minor matter, cuddling is
never about anything else and the house music
sounds hard. Are simple.

An eternal repetition

The cookies taste very sweet
My heart is beating very wild again
I missed the crossroads again
Meanwhile the old have nothing to say
The new tastes very stale
The calves got stronger
But all in all I became more tired
I still have one hope
And that has to do with joy again
When will the deep philosophy finally come
When will wisdom come
When will enlightenment come
An eternal repetition

Or everything will be fine again

The whimpering was easy to smother, it quickly became a massive inflammation and the face was no longer presentable. Give me a kiss and do not chase me with visions of the future, the evening seems cool and the TV shows a bland discussion. Get closer and don't feel at home at all today, nose is stuffy and my bald head reflects the rest of the world. Gross. Believe in a better future, read smart books about the way and fall asleep with a headache. A little happiness is in the fridge and has an expiration date. Come here and give me the remote control, I switch and believe again. The angels beam kindly at me and my full belly hangs down heavily between the chair legs. Or it will be all right again after all.

And run in circles

We shake hands
Congratulate and thank
Put our hand on the shoulder of the winner
And the heart clenches
Maybe tomorrow will be better
We'll really get involved
Everyone should like us
The opponents are squashed against the wall
And with blood they splatter innocence
We laugh at each other
And run in circles

The backpack only gets heavier

The right side of my face hung limp, first it hurt
like hell, then it twitched, and now there's no sign
of life. Having something massive on your face is
not fun. Anyone can see it and talk about it, laugh
or make fun of it. The face can be beautiful, it can
be ugly or it can be disturbed. And you open the
vastness of your soul and you can't hide anymore.
Not being able to hide tears you down. The
backpack only gets heavier.

Good sentences are not lost

The sweetheart moved through the land
Her dress fluttered around her head
The mismatched panties were showing
Go home and clear your throat
Complain your thoughts and lie too
Soon you'll be gone
You played well and became famous
Prepare for the next phase
Become lonelier and more patient
Good sentences are not lost

New supplied

Wonderful taste
Breathe unsaturated
Borrowed thoughts
Delivered feelings
Bitten off tongues
Growing desire
Briefly smiled
Badly felt
Abbreviated way
Sweet taste
Bent fingers
Healing prayers
Well placed
Gently dropped
Newly delivered

And have nothing else

Gnarled fingers grasp
The crucifix shines bright
Take a good look
Plunge into illusory reality
Another world is born
Modern wood smells pleasant
To be at home
And having nothing else

The toilet paper is used up

I feel included, trusted and accepted, opinions are coming in well, everyone is validating me and the stench is creeping out from between the door cracks. The principles sound good and whether it's enough for me I can't really say, it needs concepts, records and comparisons. I'm still too lazy and too annoyed for that at the moment. The spiritual things arrive and the world is almost endlessly filled with words, how does that work. Thinking about the latest news, and hatching new well. Have a good idea for the future and reach out. The toilet paper is used up.

And again the rule was broken

Come here now and don't lift your leg
The wishes are welcome
Beautiful voices call for the neighbor
Have a good swallow
Don't be aggressive and hit
The old fish tastes sour
And does not recognize the neuroses
Stripped and smeared
Happiness melts away
And goes back to the neighborhood
Go for a walk and despise yourself
Calm down and swallow it all down
Short requests charm
Have well said
And turn tail and disappear
Spit out the clever phrases
Go party and dance away
And the rule is broken again

A short laugh

The silence at the beginning
Well seen
Well aimed
Breaking rules
A look
One theater
Without butt
And at the beginning
And good
Everything else
Without if
The lightness
No thoughts
Old man
Also a beginning
Short laugh

And you have the sleep

My fingers, which have fallen asleep, want to reach for the switch of the bedside lamp, but I can't, they lie there cramped and feel like a uniform mass of flesh. How am I supposed to go on now, without fingers, without hands I can't find the switch, and I can't operate it. In short, is this the end or just a beginning delusion. Hope I fall asleep again and wake up fresh and awake, not in the hospital or somewhere else. Answer one more important question quickly and put the two lumps of meat under my neck. And you have the sleep.

No problem and ready

The pressure in the back of the head has increased
Clear thoughts do not exist
Living in the famous now goes now
It is just not pleasant
An iron hand stirs my brain
And the butterflies flutter excitedly
Want to have peace
Blessed peace and no noise
Rebel and vomit out the world
Repetition seems pleasant
Found it
The deep joy or happiness
You have no time
No matter and done

And yet this is also good again

The neighbor greets me kindly and gives me his
laugh, it seems very genuine and especially friendly.
We talk about the old day and survey the future,
hope for a peace and continue the world of
abundance, because it does us good. The garden is
plowed up and looks wild and untidy, regrowing
weeds will soon cover everything again. And yet
that too is good again.

Pay

Have thought of nothing and ask nothing without really saying anything or even paying.

A voracious worm fights his way through

He gets a kick in the butt
The humiliation eats a hole in your head
You become a potential killer
And forget all your well-intentioned thoughts
Your donations for a better life
Your red head gets even redder
The ego inflates
A voracious worm fights its way through

There's plenty to be happy about.

The nose is crooked
The neck looks cramped
The corners of the mouth are turned up
And everyone is happy
A hustle and bustle
Laughing, busy faces meet you
You can ask
Who can play with the ball now
It's not much of a riddle
You will solve it in peace
Not a good beginning
But a grand ending with an obituary
Don't run away
Everyone has become happy
Fall in love with a piece of the world
Don't condemn the silence inside
The hustle and bustle goes on
There is much to be happy about

At least on some days

The sour candies taste impeccable, I chew on them
and make a new plan. Since summer is already here,
I can let the cold out and think about autumn
again, about all the mosquitoes, the leeches, the
ticks and the taste of sweets. Make my opinion
count, count everything and try to accept the other
opinions, especially the beautiful and dear and
holistic opinions, radical they should not be, that's
scary. I take my favorite game in hand and distract
myself, the mouth is constantly filled with sweet
and sour, the blood sours are not yet there and I
quickly ask myself a few more questions. Then you
feel good again, not often. At least some days.

Sing a song

I have built a world
That goes well with my robe
Shined the shoes
The books carefully read
The eyes wide open
And the day fits the thoughts
Let us sing happy songs
We belong together and network
Each is proud to have the other as a friend
Our nose is stuffed and we sound nasal
Come, let's pave the way
Let the penultimate day begin
We sing a song

Be well fallen

Ran fast through the tunnel, pants wet and dirty
from deep puddles, behind me a hunchback and a
laughing devil. Hurry and flee, be good at heel and
certainly not give up. Whistling a song, it should be
a hiking song, and so it happened that I did not
really do anything against the devilish. To be well
fallen.

Losing yourself in feelings

Having found good words in the book
The words make sense
And think of a next step of meaning
Forgetting the words too quickly
In the belly it hums
Out of the mouth comes the food
The words swim away
Lose ourselves in feelings

Caught

The taste reminds us of something, the pain in the
stomach does no good, the loves are in the book,
the imagination has trapped us.

And nodded

The chants became louder and more beautiful
There was not a word to understand
Pressed my lips tightly together
And looked out of my underwear as cleverly as I
could
Innocent
I felt
It's a great chance
And nodded

A very real nod

I nodded at you diligently
And you saw it casually
Still swaying eagerly as you nodded
Lick your saliva
And nod as you do it
A very neat nod

Addicted

After going out to see the world, greeting many people, having meaningful conversations, the taste is sweet and I am hooked.

The pleasure disappears

A beautiful song sounds from the radio
The head shakes rhythmically to it
The coffee cools in the cup
The conversations fall silent
The saliva in the mouth tastes awful
The pleasure disappears

Some things are good

The soles of my feet are burning from walking around, I didn't find anything, but I was able to sweat well and in stride I increased day by day. No more waiting, but marching right away, building strength. There will be a few more days of walking, and yet the restlessness remains deep in my belly, working non-stop. Some things are good.

Have swallowed well

Thick it is in the back of the throat
The palate swells
Tried hours pass
And the pleasure does not hide
Hid for a moment
Massaged my toes
Breathed deeply
Lost the inklings
Swallowed well

And fall asleep

Serious threats touch me
Do you have the power
To teach me again
I have forgotten too much
I have swallowed
Cough well
and go to sleep

Wind up the reveries and then go out.

My first impressions after waking up were not good, too long asleep, too lopsided, violent dreams did the usual. I complained once again to the wrong person, the me, and the self-talk once again did not come to a quick end. Head talk, we all know it, triggers heart palpitations and almost kills us some days. And the reference to reality becomes harder or not harder. What reality do I mean today and pick up a new rag and stay tuned. What dreams do you have and sift through your life credits, there will be enough for the next few days. Wrap up the musings and then go out.

Erased

Listen in dismay
And say nothing
Everything sounds like it's falling apart
The brain starts to go limp
Just don't be friendly
Don't be courteous
Stay calm and cool and look tired
The switches get snuffy
Don't rush things
And everything falls apart
Then feel good
Turned on
Or
Wiped out

Really

Kisses taste sweet, the gum is already chewed all
the way through and is now soon swallowed,
swallowed well, at night the nightmares come again
and the kisses disappear, nothing is real.

Fart

A good adventure is worth its weight in gold and is
needed, is needed like uniting with God or
something. Break out, put your hands in your arms
and run laughing out loud into the next face.
Eventually they will catch them and mess up your
laughter and find an unsolvable, the famous one
from just now. The day offers many things, engine
noises, the mobility, celebrations and bread and
games. Discussions about nothing interest me,
sometimes I shout along, and yesterday I coughed
to it. The lush green of the grass already has a
calming effect on the nervous mind, fears of death
return only at night. Dear homeland, protect and
chop eaters and also protect our children. There is
still a little way and we can suppress everything,
even the smallest fart.

Now does the now no good

Was well used
The chemistry should have been right
Have been well organized
Not another word out
Wonder and marvel
Nothing lingers
Thoughts flash
Chemistry became a strong feeling
Good or not good is impossible to say
Shake hands and hold them tightly
Laugh heartily at the same time
The now is not good for the now

It often comes a quick out

Sitting at home and not feeling quite alone, waiting for the intruder and biting down on curt statements, there is also fear involved. There's a sudden creaking and pumping, you're ready to jump and you're clutching the broomstick tightly, fear plays a big part. The apartment becomes the scene, the play is heading for the climax. Have earned enough money and want to direct it in the right directions, sow and grow a lush plant. Been consumed by their own feelings, thoughts join supporting and the world no longer stands. We distribute eternity very selflessly and trust ourselves with everything. This often has a quick end.

And comes to an end

Realization is not enough
Change purifies the blood
The weeds sprout even on hot days
Better to party than to go to school
This is the world and you are human
And sorrow comes soon enough
What do we know more today
The old don't get any younger
Wear and tear makes you sway
And everything sounds good
Kind and beautiful
The sun tugs at the flowers
The colors cheer you up
You are seen
Life is good
And comes to an end

The beginning is made

Restless look at the narrowness
My hate is in my belly and grunts
You can no longer hear the whispers
My eyes are red with tears and my mouth is
crooked with laughter
The air grows cool and damp
Remains thoughtless with it
The beginning is made

The heart calms down

Be available
The environment accepts you
Eliminate the risky
Keeping the laughter good
Let yourself be treated well
Slip into romance
Breathe the humid air deeply
The heart calms down

Or lose

Seen again and again
Done evaluated
Breathed in fear for a moment
The children are sick
More and more difficult the beginning
Overstrained children fall asleep
Uncertainty spreads
And you start again and again
Or lose

One way or another

The future consists of many conversations and opinions and the believed approaching, reconsidering and falling asleep. Dreams begin and clean the past. There can also be good days, good days in the sun and good days in the womb of an illusion. Dream the day even briefly, and wake up with a sore throat and believe. Either way.

Around and but

Coming out of good reflection, pouring high
spirits, not feeling the day for a long time. The
lightness decreases with me, expels and grows
together, turns away and rubs off. Around and but.

You are already something

The suitcase is put down in the basement, it was a busy week, the travels become denser and you can not clarify anything, not even process and certainly not answer. The search for a profound conversation and going out for it, being on the road again, this time without suitcases and friendliness. The desperate attempt in the alley across the street to find the solution to melancholy, perhaps to fail, perhaps to fail everywhere and always. Looking at the feelings and noticing the aching stomach and yet being kind again and smiling and putting your hands in your pockets and starting to play. What kind of role do you like to have, are you funny and seemingly carefree, cope well with the mundanities or the serious, the tough, the one who smokes in the western and says nothing. But quickly pulls. Who do you want to be. The athlete's foot won't go away, it itches and digs deep. The cigarette is gone and the stomach still hurts. You are already something.

From the good hours

Hastened to the end
Birth there shall have been none
The stupid live well
Appearance seems alive
The belief in stories
Of the good hours

Take it all and unite

Sweet tasting cotton candy wraps you up
Lie on your back and stare at the blue sky
The world is whole and feels good
Go to sleep and dream of wild adventures
Honking builds itself into the dream and disturbs
The story gets a new direction
A thousand impressions start to narrow down
Take it all away and unite

It remains a hit

The sun is shining, the day was good, people are
sweating and the ice cream vendor has made sales.
I like to retrieve my phrases, memorize some
guiding principles and refrain from the melancholic
criticism. I bought an ice cream, my favorites
silence and melancholy were not there. Instead I
got devotion and superstition, or was it faith. And
the sun shines and the ice cream cools me down.
Life is good to me. It remains a hit.

And tomorrow comes again

To have found together and to laugh
Everything is complex and simple at the same time
When will we meet again
Revel and drink up
Senseless fraternization
We will admit some more
No one will care
The laughter will fade
And the morning will come again

Heavy

The work has brought nothing but reward, your environment has stroked the courage in you and appreciates you, the road remains the same, the stones are heavy.

Then the day would be perfect

My shirt is sweaty through and feels old, I meet friendly fellow travelers and chat about the last days, they about the last years and we meet. Being alone has its appeal, the appeal fades with the headache and dies with the dying. You dress well and are greeted, proud of many things. Proud of the mountain conquered, of the good position and of the eloquence. There we strut along and gladly shake hands with the half-poor and half-weak. We are polite and have a good style, do not lose a bad tone and do not show excitement. We air the hat, take off the sweaty shirt, shower and renew ourselves. A sublime day, there is still one important, very significant little thing missing. Then the day would be perfect.

Simply promised

Close your eyes and open your heart
Did I perceive the magic
The toes glow in the sun
The taste in my mouth feels better
The wind blows through my armpits
The battle is not happily fought
And still smile
Secretly and bashfully
Throw me into the grass
Nothing was promised
Simply promised

Where is the final written

Late at night reflect on the day
Smell the leaf and take a deep breath
Glide into another dimension
Perceive a high pleasant sound
Cough briefly and spit out the phlegm
Have smoked too much
Forget the covered
Letting the soul be
Where is the last written

Murderer

Questioningly, the slightly bruised fish eye of the dead fish looks at you and feels good about it, who are you in it, a fisherman or are you a murderer.

And why don't you admit yourself

The thoughts sink slowly
Teeth have already fallen out
Conversations with neighbors sound confused
We are all on the verge of death
And eagerly strive for sentimentality
The last song is sung
No one wants to start right
And why don't you admit

Why not

My heart is heavy The air is thin. The breath stops.
Children laugh. Time passes much faster. An
assumption has become a certainty. And it is
wrong. All ideas are to be forgotten, carry nothing.
I turn on the light, the room becomes pleasantly
bright. Why not.